Especially for kids and their

The Mini

Book of Presidents

by Betty Debnam

D0735578

Andrews and McMeel
A Universal Press Syndicate Company
Kansas City

Contents

George Washington

(1732-1799)

State born: Virginia
Served: 1789-1797
Occupation: farmer
Party: Federalist

George Washington is called "The Father of our Country."

George Washington was our military leader during the War of Independence. He served as chairman of the convention that wrote our Constitution. He served our country well in his two terms as our first president. He was first sworn into office on April 30, 1787.

George Washington married Martha Custis, a wealthy widow. He raised her two children as his own. He died at his home, Mount Vernon, in Virginia.

George Washington

John Adams

(1735-1826)

State born: Massachusetts
Served: 1797-1801
Occupation: lawyer
Party: Federalist

John Adams was a leader of the American Revolution and an outstanding founding father.

He was appointed to the committee to help draft the Declaration of Independence. He helped guide it through the Continental Congress.

John Adams also served as a diplomat in France and England.

He was the first president to live in the White House.

His wife, Abigail, was the only woman in U.S. history to be the wife of one president and the mother of another. Their son, John Quincy, served as our sixth president.

John Adams

John Adams

Thomas Jefferson

(1743-1826)

State born: Virginia
Served: 1801-1809
Occupation: planter, lawyer
Party: Democratic-Republican*

Thomas Jefferson is one of history's most outstanding men.

He was the author of the Declaration of Independence.

He also served as governor of Virginia, minister to France, secretary of state, vice president and then president.

While he was president, our country doubled in size because of the Louisiana Purchase.

He founded the University of Virginia. Thousands of tourists visit his home, Monticello, each year.

*Jefferson and Madison founded this party which later became the Democratic Party.

Thomas Jefferson

James Madison

(1751-1836)

State born: Virginia
Served: 1809-1817
Occupation: lawyer
Party: Democratic-Republican*

James Madison is called "The Father of our Constitution." More than any delegate, he influenced what went on at the Constitutional Convention.

He later served in the House of Representatives and helped write the Bill of Rights.

He also served as secretary of state under Thomas Jefferson.

Madison was president during the unpopular War of 1812 when the British occupied Washington.

His wife, Dolley, was a famous Washington hostess.

*Madison and Jefferson founded this party, which later became the Democratic Party.

James Madison

James Monroe

(1758-1831)

State born: Virginia
Served: 1817-1825
Occupation: lawyer
Party: Democratic-Republican*

James Monroe is most famous for the Monroe Doctrine. This doctrine warned European countries not to try and take over the government of any countries in our part of the world, the Western Hemisphere.

Monroe was a lifelong friend of Thomas Jefferson. He served as a soldier in the Revolutionary War. He also served as a U.S. senator, minister to France and governor of Virginia.

*This party later became the Democratic Party.

James Monroe

John Quincy Adams

(1767-1848)

State born: Massachusetts
Served: 1825-1829
Occupation: lawyer
Party: Democratic-Republican*

John Quincy Adams was the only president who was the son of another. His father was John Adams, our second president.

John Quincy Adams was an outstanding diplomat. He served as secretary of state before becoming president.

He thought the government should encourage the arts and sciences, and sponsored the founding of the Smithsonian Institution.

Adams lost his bid for re-election. He later became the only ex-president to be elected to the House of Representatives, where he served for 17 years.

*This party later became the Democratic Party.

John Quincy Adams

John Quincy Adams

Andrew Jackson

(1767-1845)

State born: South Carolina
Served: 1829-1837
Occupation: lawyer
Party: Democratic

Andrew Jackson was the first president born in a log cabin. He was a man of the frontier who sought to represent the common man. He was called "Old Hickory" because he was so tough.

Jackson became a successful lawyer and planter in Tennessee. He served in both houses of Congress. He gained fame as a military hero and Indian fighter.

When he ran for re-election in 1832, he became the first president to be nominated by a political convention. Before that time, presidents were mostly nominated by state legislatures. Under his leadership the Democratic-Republican Party was changed into the Democratic Party.

Andrew Jackson

Martin Van Buren

(1782-1862)

State born: New York
Served: 1837-1841
Occupation: lawyer
Party: Democratic

Martin Van Buren was born in 1782 in Kinderhook, N.Y.

He became a lawyer. He never remarried after his wife of 12 years died.

He served as a U.S. senator and as governor of New York. He served as vice president under Andrew Jackson.

Van Buren became president in 1837. Three months later, our country went into a depression. His efforts to improve things failed. However, he was successful in foreign affairs. He was against slavery. He opposed letting Texas join the Union because it would add another slave state. He ran for president two more times but lost in both tries.

Martin Van Buren

William Henry Harrison

(1773-1841)

State born: Virginia
Served: 1841
Occupation: farmer
Party: Whig*

William Henry Harrison was the first president to die in office. He caught a cold on his Inauguration Day and died of pneumonia 30 days later. (His grandson, Benjamin, became the 23rd president.)

Harrison was born in Virginia, the son of a well-to-do planter. When he grew up, he settled in North Bend, Ohio.

He became a congressman and later a senator. He also served as minister to Colombia.

He gained fame as an Indian fighter and an Army general in the War of 1812.

He used the slogan "Tippecanoe and Tyler Too" in his election campaign. Tippecanoe was an Indian battle he won. John Tyler was his vice presidential running mate.

* This party was active for about 30 years.

William Henry Harrison

John Tyler

(1790-1862)

State born: Virginia
Served: 1841-1845
Occupation: lawyer
Party: Whig*

William Henry Harrison died a month after taking office. John Tyler became the first vice president to become president because of the death of the man elected to the job.

While some people suggested that he be only an "acting president," Tyler took the office very seriously. He often clashed with Congress and his own party.

One of the most important things he did was to pave the way for Texas to join the Union.

Tyler's father was a well-to-do planter. Before becoming president, Tyler served in the U.S. House of Representatives, as governor of Virginia and in the U.S. Senate. He married twice and had a total of 15 children.

* This party was active for about 30 years.

John Tyler

John Tyler

James K. Polk

(1795-1849)

State born: North Carolina
Served: 1845-1849
Occupation: lawyer
Party: Democratic

James K. Polk was born in a log house near Charlotte, N.C. He was the oldest of 10 children. When he was 11, the family moved to Tennessee where his father became a successful farmer.

Polk became a lawyer and served in the U.S. House of Representatives. He later became governor of Tennessee.

Under Polk, our country grew more than it had at any time in its history. It grew to stretch from the Atlantic to the Pacific. During his term, we fought a successful war with Mexico over California. Our country was very prosperous during his four years.

He and his wife, Sarah, had no children. She was a deeply religious woman who served as her husband's secretary.

Polk chose not to run for a second term.

He died less than three months after he left office.

James K. Polk

Zachary Taylor

(1784-1850)

State born: Virginia
Served: 1849-1850
Occupation: soldier
Party: Whig*

Zachary Taylor was the first professional soldier to become president. He was called "Old Rough and Ready" because he never lost a battle in his 40-year military career.

Taylor was born in Virginia. He was educated by tutors. His father was a farmer.

Taylor was a Southerner and a slaveholder. However, he fought against slavery in the new western areas that were being added to our growing country.

Taylor served only 16 months of his term. He died in office at the age of 65.

* This party was active for about 30 years.

26

Zachary Taylor

Millard Fillmore

(1800-1874)

State born: New York
Served: 1850-1853
Occupation: teacher, lawyer
Party: Whig*

When Zachary Taylor died in office, his vice president, Millard Fillmore, became president.

Fillmore was born into a very poor family. Growing up, he did not get much education, but worked on his family farm. When he was 18 he was tutored by a young teacher, whom he later married. He studied law and became a lawyer. He was elected to the U.S. House of Representatives.

As president, Fillmore helped work out a compromise on slavery that prevented a civil war for more than 10 years.

* This party was active for about 30 years.

Millard Fillmore

Franklin Pierce

(1804-1869)

State born: New Hampshire
Served: 1853-1857
Occupation: lawyer
Party: Democratic

While Franklin Pierce was president, the country was very prosperous but very divided on slavery. He was a friend of the Southern cause. Because of this, he made many enemies.

Before becoming president, Pierce served in the House of Representatives and also in the Senate.

As president, Pierce tried to annex (add on) Hawaii and Cuba to the United States. These plans fell through. While he was president, the United States bought land from Mexico, making our country larger. This land became the southern parts of New Mexico and Arizona.

Franklin Pierce

James Buchanan

(1791-1868)

State born: Pennsylvania
Served: 1857-1861
Occupation: lawyer
Party: Democratic

James Buchanan was our president in the years just before the Civil War. He was against slavery. However, the laws at that time protected slavery so he did not fight against it.

Buchanan was born in a log cabin. His father ran a country store. Young Buchanan grew up to be a successful lawyer.

Before becoming president he had served in both houses of Congress. He also served as secretary of state and ambassador to Russia.

Buchanan is our only president who never married.

James Buchanan

Abraham Lincoln

(1809-1865)

State born: Kentucky
Served: 1861-1865
Occupation: lawyer
Party: Republican

Abraham Lincoln was a great president. His leadership during the Civil War preserved our Union and ended slavery.

Lincoln was born in a log cabin in Kentucky. He went to school for less than a year while he was growing up. He taught himself by reading many borrowed books.

Lincoln settled in Illinois and became a lawyer. He married Mary Todd. They had four children.

Lincoln was elected to the U.S. Congress. He became our first Republican president.

The Civil War ended in victory for the North on April 9, 1865. Lincoln was shot on April 14 and died one day later.

Abraham Lincoln

Abraham Lincoln

Andrew Johnson

(1808-1875)

State born: North Carolina
Served: 1865-1869
Occupation: tailor
Party: Democratic

Johnson became president when Lincoln was assassinated. He is our only president to be nearly removed from office by Congress. Many congressmen were against him. He and Congress fought over many issues, particularly on how to treat the South after the Civil War. Johnson was impeached (which means he was formally accused) by the House of Representatives; he was put on trial and acquitted (cleared) by the Senate and was allowed to finish his term.

Johnson had come from a very poor family.

He went to work for a tailor when he was 13. He ran away to Tennessee two years later. He became a successful tailor. His wife taught him to write.

Before becoming president, Johnson served as a U.S. representative, governor of Tennessee and a U.S. senator. He is the only person to be elected to the U.S. Senate after serving as president.

Andrew Johnson

Ulysses S. Grant

(1822-1885)

State born: Ohio
Served: 1869-1877
Occupation: soldier
Party: Republican

Ulysses S. Grant was the son of a farmer who ran a tannery.* He went to West Point but resigned from the Army nine years later. He went back into service when the Civil War started. He became a famous military hero and commander of the Union armies.

Grant was not as good a president as he was a soldier. There were many scandals during his two terms. Grant was a very honest man, and was never involved in the scandals. However, many consider him a very weak president.

*A tannery is a business that turns hides into leather.

Ulysses S. Grant

Rutherford B. Hayes

(1822-1893)

State born: Ohio
Served: 1877-1881
Occupation: lawyer
Party: Republican

Rutherford B. Hayes won the presidency in the most bitterly contested election in the U.S. history. He won by only one electoral vote.

Before he became president, Hayes had served as a Union general in the Civil War, a U.S. representative and governor of Ohio.

As president, he withdrew federal troops from the South. This created a better feeling between the North and South.

While Hayes was president, the country continued to grow and many factories were built.

Hayes and his wife, Lucy, started the custom of the Easter egg roll on the White House lawn.

Rutherford B. Hayes

James A. Garfield

(1831-1881)

State born: Ohio
Served: 1881
Occupation: teacher, lawyer
Party: Republican

James Garfield was assassinated only a few months after he became president. He was killed by a man who did not get the job he wanted. Garfield was our second president to be assassinated.

Garfield was the last president born in a log cabin. He worked hard to send himself through college. He later became president of a college and a lawyer. He became a general for the Union forces in the Civil War.

Garfield was elected to the U.S. House of Representatives eight times. It took 36 ballots for him to win the Republican nomination for president.

Garfield sometimes entertained guests by writing Latin with one hand and Greek with the other.

James A. Garfield.

James A. Garfield

Chester A. Arthur

(1830-1886)

State born: Vermont
Served: 1881-1885
Occupation: teacher, lawyer
Party: Republican

Chester A. Arthur became president when James Garfield died of a bullet wound. He was the fourth vice president to take over after the death of a president.

Arthur was never elected to any office except vice president. He was a powerful politician who gained his support by helping his party win elections.

As president, Arthur became known for his honesty. Before he took office, many people were given government jobs in return for favors. Congress passed a law, called the Civil Service Act, to stop this. Arthur did what he could to enforce the law. He made many enemies and did not get re-elected.

Chester A. Arthur

Grover Cleveland

(1837-1908)

State born: New Jersey
Served: 1885-1889, 1893-1897
Occupation: lawyer
Party: Democratic

Grover Cleveland is our only president to serve two terms that were not in a row. He served one term, then lost to Republican Benjamin Harrison. Four years later, in 1893, he defeated Harrison and was re-elected.

Before he became president, Cleveland served as a sheriff, mayor of Buffalo, N.Y. and governor of New York.

He was known for his honesty. He tried to heal the wounds of the Civil War by treating the South more kindly.

Cleveland married Frances Folsom in 1886. He is the only president to be wed in the White House. They had five children.

Grover Cleveland

Benjamin Harrison

(1833-1901)

State born: Ohio
Served: 1889-1893
Occupation: lawyer
Party: Republican

Benjamin Harrison was the only grandson of a president to become a president. His grandfather was William Henry Harrison.

Benjamin Harrison's father was a well-to-do farmer. Benjamin became famous as a lawyer, soldier and politician. He moved from Ohio to Indiana.

As president, Harrison worked to gain respect for our flag. He ordered that it be flown over all government buildings.

While he was president, six new states joined the Union.

Harrison lost his bid for re-election to Grover Cleveland, whom he had defeated the first time he ran.

Benjamin Harrison

William McKinley

(1843-1901)

State born: Ohio
Served: 1897-1901
Occupation: lawyer
Party: Republican

Under the leadership of McKinley, our country became a world power. We won the Spanish-American War. We also added Hawaii, Puerto Rico, Guam, the Philippines and American Samoa.

Before becoming president, McKinley served as an officer in the Union Army, as governor of Ohio and as a U.S. congressman.

He was devoted to his wife, who became an invalid after they married.

McKinley was our third president to be assassinated. He was shot on September 6, 1901. He had served six months of his second term.

William McKinley

Theodore Roosevelt

(1858-1919)

State born: New York
Served: 1901-1909
Occupation: writer, politician
Party: Republican

Theodore Roosevelt was born into an important and wealthy family in New York City.

"Teddy" Roosevelt was only 42 when he became president.

Roosevelt was a popular leader who believed in strong armed forces. His motto was: "Speak softly and carry a big stick." He also worked to save our natural resources. He fought to break up big, powerful companies.

While he was president, building of the Panama Canal started.

Roosevelt left office in 1909. He lost when he ran for president as a third-party candidate in 1912.

Theodore Roosevelt

William Howard Taft

(1857-1930)

State born: Ohio
Served: 1909-1913
Occupation: lawyer
Party: Republican

William Howard Taft did not want to be president. He ran because Theodore Roosevelt asked him to.

Before becoming president, Taft served as a judge and as governor of the Philippines. Taft was our country's largest president. He was 6 feet tall and weighed over 300 pounds.

As president, he fought to conserve our natural resources. He was successful in getting many laws passed. However, he lost his bid for re-election.

He later became the only ex-president to be appointed to the U.S. Supreme Court. He served as chief justice from 1921-1930.

William Howard Taft

Woodrow Wilson

(1856-1924)

State born: Virginia
Served: 1913-1921
Occupation: lawyer, educator
Party: Democratic

Before becoming president, Woodrow Wilson was a Princeton university professor and later governor of New Jersey.

As president, he curbed the power of big businesses and carried out many reforms.

Wilson tried to keep our country out of World War I, but could not. After the war, he worked to get our country to join the League of Nations. This group is much like our United Nations of today. Congress defeated this idea. In 1919, Wilson suffered a stroke 17 months before the end of his second term. He died in 1924.

Woodrow Wilson

Warren G. Harding

(1865-1923)

State born: Ohio
Served: 1921-1923
Occupation: newspaper editor
Party: Republican

Warren G. Harding is the only newspaper editor to be elected president. He had served as a U.S. senator before his election.

Harding was elected during the early 1920s. He promised to return the country to the good old days of an earlier and quieter America. This was a very hard thing to do during the Roaring '20s.

Many people think of Harding as our weakest president. Some of the people whom he appointed to important jobs were dishonest. There were many scandals.

Harding died in office halfway through his term.

Warren G. Harding

Calvin Coolidge

(1872-1933)

State born: Vermont
Served: 1923-1929
Occupation: lawyer
Party: Republican

Calvin Coolidge became president when President Harding died in office in 1923. He was later elected to a full term in 1924. He was an honest man who was known for his common sense. He was also known as "Silent Cal" because he was a man of very few words.

Although he was popular, he chose not to run for a second term in 1928.

Before becoming president, Coolidge had served as governor of Massachusetts.

Coolidge believed that government should not interfere with business. He was in office during the Roaring '20s when times were good. Some of his policies led to the Great Depression.

Calvin Coolidge

Herbert C. Hoover

(1874-1964)

State born: Iowa
Served: 1929-1933
Occupation: engineer
Party: Republican

Herbert Hoover was our president during the start of the Great Depression. Seven months after he took office, the stock market crashed.

Many people blamed him when their businesses failed and when they lost their homes. He was defeated by a wide margin when he ran for re-election.

Hoover was a self-made man. He worked his way through college and became a mining engineer. He made a fortune in gold.

After he left office, he served our country in many ways. By the time he died in 1964, he had regained the respect of his countrymen.

Herbert C. Hoover

Franklin D. Roosevelt

(1882-1945)

State born: New York
Served: 1933-1945
Occupation: lawyer, politician
Party: Democratic

Franklin Delano Roosevelt served as president of our country longer than any other man (12 years). He is considered one of our greatest presidents.

Roosevelt was from a wealthy family.

In 1921, he was stricken by polio, which left him handicapped, but he did not give up.

Since it was difficult for him to travel, his wife, Eleanor, represented him on many occasions. She became a very famous lady.

As president, Roosevelt took action to help end the Great Depression. His programs were called the "New Deal." He led our country during most of World War II.

He died in April 1945, only three months after beginning his fourth term.

Franklin D. Roosevelt

Harry S Truman

(1884-1972)

State born: Missouri
Served: 1945-1953
Occupation: politician
Party: Democratic

Harry Truman became president when Franklin Roosevelt died. Truman was not a college graduate. Before being elected, he had run a clothing store and served as a county judge and a U.S. senator.

As president, Truman made many important decisions. Shortly after he took office, he made the decision to drop the atomic bomb on Japan. This forced the Japanese to surrender and ended World War II.

He also started a program giving aid to countries who were against communism. Another of his programs gave aid to countries damaged by World War II.

Harry S Truman

Dwight D. Eisenhower

(1890-1969)

State born: Texas
Served: 1953-1961
Occupation: soldier
Party: Republican

Dwight D. Eisenhower became famous as commander of the troops in Europe during World War II. After the war, he became president of Columbia University.

At first, Eisenhower said "no" to people who wanted him to run for president. But he changed his mind and became the first Republican president to be elected in 20 years. "I Like Ike" was his campaign slogan.

Shortly after taking office, he took steps to end the Korean War. He worked hard for peace around the world. While he was in office, we launched our first space satellite.

Eisenhower believed strongly in equal rights for all of our citizens. He served two terms.

Dwight D. Eisenhower

John F. Kennedy

(1917-1963)

State born: Massachusetts
Served: 1961-1963
Occupation: politician
Party: Democratic

At the age of 43, John Fitzgerald Kennedy was the youngest man ever elected president. He was also the youngest to die in office. He was shot and killed two years and 10 months later, on November 22, 1963, in Dallas.

Kennedy was from a large and wealthy family. While serving in the Navy in World War II, he became a war hero. He showed great courage when his patrol boat was sunk in the South Pacific.

Before becoming president, he served as a U.S. representative and a senator.

While Kennedy was president, he forced the Russians to withdraw missiles from Cuba. The United States launched its first man into space. Kennedy also set up the Peace Corps.

John F. Kennedy

Lyndon B. Johnson

(1908-1973)

State born: Texas
Served: 1963-1969
Occupation: elementary teacher, politician
Party: Democratic

Lyndon Baines Johnson became president when John Kennedy was assassinated.

Johnson was from a political family in Texas. His father served in the Texas Legislature.

Before becoming president, Johnson had served as a U.S. representative and U.S. senator. He was an outstanding leader.

While he was president, he pushed laws dealing with civil rights. He also pushed through laws to help the poor. He called these his War on Poverty.

When the war in Vietnam dragged on, Johnson became unpopular. He decided not to seek re-election for a second term.

Lyndon B. Johnson

Richard Nixon

(1913-1994)

State born: California
Served: 1969-1974
Occupation: lawyer
Party: Republican

Richard Nixon is the only president ever to resign. He was involved in what was called the "Watergate" scandal. This involved illegal burglaries of the Democratic headquarters during his second election campaign.

While Nixon claimed that he was not involved, many of his aides went to prison for their part in it.

Before becoming president, Nixon served as a U.S. representative and a senator from California. He also served as vice president under Eisenhower.

As a president, Nixon withdrew American troops from Vietnam. He also improved our relations with China and other countries.

Richard Nixon

Gerald R. Ford

(1913-)

State born: Nebraska
Served: 1974-1977
Occupation: lawyer
Party: Republican

Gerald Ford is the only person to serve as vice president and president of the United States without ever being elected to either office.

Ford was appointed to the office of vice president by Nixon. He succeeded Spiro Agnew, who was forced to resign. Ford had served as vice president for only eight months when he took over as president after Richard Nixon was forced to resign.

Before becoming vice president, Ford had served as a U.S. representative in Congress from Michigan for 13 terms.

Because of many problems such as inflation and unemployment, Ford lost his bid for election to a full term.

Gerald R. Ford

Jimmy Carter

(1924-)

State born: Georgia
Served: 1977-1981
Occupation: farmer, naval officer
Party: Democratic

Jimmy Carter's real name is James Earl Carter, but he always wanted to be called Jimmy.

Before becoming president, he served as an officer in the Navy, ran his family's peanut business and served as governor of Georgia.

Jimmy Carter worked hard for human rights for people around the world. He helped to improve relations between Israel and Egypt at the Camp David Peace Conference. He lost a lot of his popularity when American hostages were seized in Iran in 1979. He was unable to gain their freedom. He lost in his bid for re-election.

Jimmy Carter

Ronald Reagan

(1911-)

State born: Illinois
Served: 1981-1989
Occupation: actor
Party: Republican

Before becoming president, Ronald Reagan had been an actor for about 30 years and served as governor of California for two terms. At the age of 69, he was the oldest man ever to be elected to the office of president. He became one of our most popular presidents ever.

As president, he cut taxes and raised the amount spent for defense. He also brought inflation and unemployment under control. He brought about friendlier relations with the Soviet Union. He worked to fight the spread of communism in Latin America.

Ronald Reagan

George Bush

(1924-)

State born: Massachusetts
Served: 1989-1993
Occupation: oil businessman, politician
Party: Republican

George Herbert Walker Bush served two terms as vice president when Ronald Reagan was president.

Before becoming president, he had also served as director of the CIA, ambassador to China and a congressman from Texas. He had also been a successful oil businessman.

Bush is from a wealthy family. His father, Prescott Bush, was a U.S. senator from Connecticut.

First lady Barbara Bush is very interested in helping kids—and adults, too—learn to read.

When Kuwait was invaded by Iraq in 1990, Bush worked with the United Nations to organize Operation Desert Storm. This joint effort freed Kuwait in 1991.

George Bush

Bill Clinton

(1946-)

State born: Arkansas
Served: 1993-2001
Occupation: lawyer
Party: Democrat

Bill Clinton began thinking of running for president even when he was a teenager.

He went to college at Georgetown University in Washington, D.C. He won a Rhodes scholarship to study at Oxford University in England. He later graduated from Yale Law School. He returned to Arkansas to become a law professor.

By the time he was 30, he was elected attorney general of Arkansas.

He was only 32 when he became the youngest governor of any state. He lost the next election but ran again two years later and won. He was elected to a total of five terms as governor of Arkansas.

His wife Hillary played an important part in his successful campaign. The Clintons have one daughter, Chelsea.

He enjoys playing the saxophone.

Bill Clinton

George W. Bush

(1946-)

State born: Texas
Served: 2001-
Occupation: businessman
Party: Republican

George Bush is the second president to be the son of a president. His father, George Bush, was our 41st president.

Bush studied at Yale University and Harvard Business School.

He was a pilot in the Texas Air National Guard. Before entering politics, he worked in the oil and gas business. He was also part-owner of the Texas Rangers baseball team.

He entered politics in 1978 when he ran for the U.S. House of Representatives, but lost the election. He then worked as an adviser on his father's campaign for vice president under Ronald Reagan.

In 1994, Bush re-entered politics and was elected governor of Texas. He was re-elected in 1998.

He and his wife, Laura, a former school librarian, have twin daughters, Jenna and Barbara.

George W. Bush

The Electoral Vote
Electing Our President and Vice President

Our president and vice president are chosen by the Electoral College. This is not a college with students and a campus.

Another meaning for "college" is a group that meets and has special duties.

The Electoral College has the duty to elect our top two leaders. This plan for electing the president and vice president was set down in our Constitution. Here's how it works.

THE WINNER TAKES ALL.

NC HAS 13 ELECTORAL VOTES

When citizens vote, their votes make up what is called the "popular" vote.

The popular vote is the first step in electing a president.

The candidate with the biggest popular vote in a state wins all of that state's electoral votes.

The people who cast these votes are called "electors."

The political parties in each state nominate a set of electors equal to that state's number of senators and representatives.

If a state has three people in Congress, it would nominate a set of 3 Republican electors and a set of 3 Democratic electors.

If an independent is running for president, he or she would nominate a set of electors, too.

There are in total 538 electors.

Number of senators 100
Number of representatives 435
From the District of Columbia 3

A candidate needs 270 electoral votes to win.

We all know on election night who won by counting the electoral votes.

However, we go through two more steps.

In December, the winning electors from every state

meet in their state capitals and cast their electoral votes.

They are expected to automatically vote for their party's choice.

These votes are put in sealed envelopes and sent to the president of the U.S. Senate.

On January 6, the president of the Senate opens the envelopes. He reads them before a meeting of the U.S. Senate and House of Representatives.

If there is a tie or if no one gets 270 votes, then the U.S. House of Representatives must decide who will be the next president. The U.S. Senate then would select the vice president.

This has happened only twice in our country's history, in 1800 and 1824.

Political Words

Here are the definitions of some terms that will help you understand elections:

Politics (POL-e-tiks): all about elections and how we govern ourselves.

Term: the number of years that a president serves (four). We elect our presidents in even years, every four years.

Politicians (pol-e-TISH-ens) are people who try to win elections.

Political party: a group that tries to control the government by winning elections. The big political parties are the Republicans and the Democrats. Our Constitution does not mention political parties. Through the years they came into being.

George Washington did not believe in political parties. He thought that candidates should not ask for votes. They should wait to be selected.

Political cartoon: a drawing showing the artist's reaction to a political news event. The donkey and the elephant first appeared in political cartoons more than 100 years ago. The first Democratic donkey cartoon appeared in 1828. The first Republican elephant cartoon appeared in 1874.

The Democratic donkey

The Republican elephant

Political campaign: a contest for a political office or job.

Run for office: to campaign for an office.

The first president to campaign by car was William Howard Taft in 1912. Before that time, candidates traveled by horse, buggy and train. Today, they often travel by jet.

The first president to use radio to reach Americans at home was Franklin Roosevelt. His talks were called "fireside chats." Today's candidates often use TV.

The White House

The White House has 132 rooms. The main building is the oldest part. The two wings were added later.

A. East Wing with tour and military aides' offices.
B. Long hall with windows. A movie theater is along this hall.
C. Main building.
D. Long hall with offices for the press.
E. The Oval Office or president's office.
F. Executive offices for the president's staff.

After a new president is sworn into office, he moves to the house that goes with the job.

While the White House is furnished, new first families bring in some of their own furniture.

Each first lady redecorates the family rooms on the second and third floors as she wishes.

A special committee helps her if she wants to change anything in the rooms that are open to the public.

To find out about the White House, we talked with an expert, William Seale. He spent 10 years writing a book for adults about the White House.

Mini Page: *How old is the White House?*

Mr. Seale: The White House was built in 1800. John Adams, the first president to live there, moved in November 1, 1800. It was designed by an Irish immigrant, James Hoban.

George Washington insisted that the house be of stone. He is the man who built the house. He gave the orders and approved the plans. He wanted it to stand for ages, just as he wanted the nation to stand for ages. He lived to see the building finished but he never lived in it. He is the only president who never did.

Mini Page: *What is it like to live in the White House?*

Mr. Seale: Living in the White House is like living in a very elegant hotel where you are the only resident and where the hotel is a home. Everything that goes on centers around the president and the first lady. It is very convenient and very beautiful. One gets used to all that service. However, there is not a lot of privacy.

White House Workers

About 91 people look after the White House's public and private rooms and serve the first family. These include:

Chief usher, who oversees the staff.

Curator, who looks after the furnishing and art collection.

Butlers

Carpenters

Chefs

Doormen

Electricians

Gardeners and flower designers

Operations crews, who put up ropes and move furniture.

Painters

White House Rooms on Tour

Here are the rooms on the tour. Some rooms are named for their color.

1. The Library
2. The Vermeil Room
3. The China Room
4. The Diplomatic Reception Room
5. The East Room
6. The Green Room
7. The Blue Room
8. The Red Boom
9. The State Dining Room

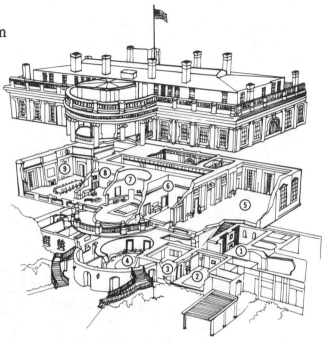

The White House is one of the biggest tourist attractions in the country. More than a million and a half people tour it each year. If you want to get on a special tour contact your congressman. A few of the public rooms are on the tour. The president's living quarters are not. People who want to take the tour can go to the White House on that same day and pick up tickets while they last. Or they can contact their congressman and ask for tour tickets for a certain date.

The East Room is the biggest room in the White House. It has been used for dances, concerts, weddings, church services and other big occasions.

The President Wears Many Hats!

Chief executive

As chief executive, the president is the boss of millions of U.S. government employees. He also must propose laws to Congress that he thinks should be passed.

Economic leader

As economic leader, the president has to keep prices from going up and up. He also must keep our businesses active and our workers on the job.

Commander in chief

As commander in chief, the president is in charge of our Navy, Marines, Air Force, Coast Guard and Army. He must see that our armed forces are ready for combat.

Chief diplomat

As chief diplomat, the president helps decide how our country will act toward other countries. He picks the ambassadors, whom the Senate must approve.

Chief of state

As chief of state, the president represents our country here and in other lands. He attends many ceremonies as a representative and symbol of the United States. A king might carry out these duties in other countries.

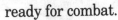

Party leader

As party leader, the president has much influence over the way his political party thinks about national problems. He also makes speeches and tries to raise money for his party.

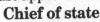